DA

2-11-09

4-15-09

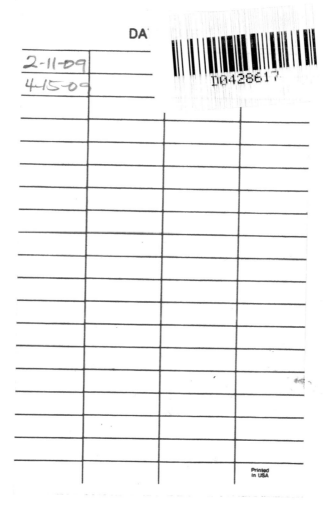

D0428617

Printed
in USA

Isaac Newton

Isaac Newton

By Kathleen Krull

Illustrated by Boris Kulikov

Viking

VIKING

Published by Penguin Group

Penguin Young Readers Group, 345 Hudson Street, New York, New York 10014, U.S.A.

Penguin Group (Canada), 90 Eglinton Avenue East, Suite 700, Toronto, Ontario, Canada M4P 2Y3
(a division of Pearson Penguin Canada Inc.)

Penguin Books Ltd, 80 Strand, London WC2R 0RL, England

Penguin Ireland, 25 St Stephen's Green, Dublin 2, Ireland (a division of Penguin Books Ltd)

Penguin Group (Australia), 250 Camberwell Road, Camberwell, Victoria 3124, Australia
(a division of Pearson Australia Group Pty Ltd)

Penguin Books India Pvt Ltd, 11 Community Centre, Panchsheel Park, New Delhi - 110 017, India

Penguin Group (NZ), Cnr Airborne and Rosedale Roads, Albany, Auckland 1310, New Zealand
(a division of Pearson New Zealand Ltd)

Penguin Books (South Africa) (Pty) Ltd, 24 Sturdee Avenue, Rosebank, Johannesburg 2196, South Africa

Penguin Books Ltd, Registered Offices: 80 Strand, London WC2R 0RL, England

First published in 2006 by Viking, a division of Penguin Young Readers Group

5 7 9 10 8 6 4

Text copyright © Kathleen Krull, 2006
Illustrations copyright © Boris Kulikov, 2006
All rights reserved

LIBRARY OF CONGRESS CATALOGING-IN-PUBLICATION DATA
Krull, Kathleen.
Isaac Newton / by Kathleen Krull ; [Boris Kulikov, illustrator].
p. cm. — (Giants of science)
Includes bibliographical references and index.
ISBN 0-670-05921-8
1. Newton, Isaac, Sir, 1642-1727—Juvenile literature. 2. Physicists—Great Britain—Biography—Juvenile
literature. I. Kulikov, Boris, date- ill. II. Title.
QC16.N7K78 2006
530'.092—dc22
2005017741

Printed in U.S.A.   •   Set in KennerlyH   •   Book design by Jim Hoover

To Rubin Pfeffer, belatedly—K.K.

Acknowledgments
For help with research, the author thanks
Robert Burnham and Patricia Laughlin, Patricia Daniels,
Dr. Lawrence M. Principe, Susan Cohen, Gary Brewer,
Dr. Helen Foster James and Dr. Bob James, Sheila Cole,
Janet Pascal, Gery Greer, and Bob Ruddick—and most
of all to Jane O'Connor.

CONTENTS

Isaac Newton

INTRODUCTION

"If I have seen further [than other people]
it is by standing upon the shoulders of giants."

—Isaac Newton, 1675

ECRETIVE, WITHDRAWN, OBSESSIVE.
Ruthless, bitter, perhaps in need of therapy. . . .
All these things apply to Isaac Newton. Oh, and
he was one of the greatest scientific minds of all time.
(Albert Einstein, who should know, said Newton was
the greatest.)

In Newton's day—late seventeenth-century
England—the word "scientist" hadn't come into
use yet and wouldn't for another 150 years.
Newton was known as a "natural philosopher,"
someone interested in discovering why the world

works the way it does. His discoveries were huge: He invented a new system of mathematics (calcu-lus); he created the reflecting telescope, which uses mirrors instead of lenses; and he figured out the principle of gravity, linking the motion of planets to familiar things like the falling of apples. He described the basic laws of motion that underlie all of physics. Newton showed that the universe operates on mathematical principles. His laws give reasons why planets move as they do. He even helped change the way scientists work, by relying on experiments and testing to bear out his ideas—what we now call the scientific method.

How did he do all this? In an exchange of let-ters with one of his many enemies—another very accomplished scientist named Robert Hooke—Newton tried to explain. He was able to see fur-ther, he said, because he stood on "the shoulders of giants." In other words, he had benefitted from the discoveries of others before him.

But nothing with Isaac Newton was ever straightforward, including this explanation. At first, the remark sounds like a compliment, Newton implying that Hooke was also a giant. But Hooke was his enemy, so some biographers think that the words are, instead, indirectly making fun of Hooke, who was unusually short. Or perhaps Newton was being phony, falsely modest in the same insincere way he signed his letters to Hooke "your real friend and humble servant"?

Whatever Newton's underlying motive, the quote still offers a beautifully worded summary of how science progresses. One person builds on the work of others. It became one of his most famous statements—Newton the genius, admitting his debts to other geniuses. So who were the "giants" who preceded him—whose shoulders did he stand on? Many other people's—including Robert Hooke's.

The world of Newton's day vibrated with change and drama. English politics, for example, was like an extreme sport—kings coming and going, getting beheaded, being run out of the country. Newton seemed to float above the fray. Up in his ivory tower at Cambridge University, he lived a quiet life. A life apart.

Except when he was poking sharp objects into his eyes, throwing world-class tantrums, burning fires night and day in his secret laboratory, and making earth-shattering discoveries and refusing to tell anyone.

And the story about Newton and the apple? It's true . . . at least Isaac Newton said so.

CHAPTER ONE

All Alone

"GRIM" IS A FITTING description for Isaac Newton's childhood. It began on Christmas Day, 1642.

It wasn't a time for celebration. His father had died three months earlier. A premature infant, Isaac was so tiny that no one expected him to make it. The story is that for the first few days, his mother, Hannah, put him in a little box behind the wood-stove to keep him warm. A special pillow fit around his neck to prop up his wobbly head.

In the 1600s, women in England often had twelve

or more children, usually with only half surviving to adulthood. But little Isaac Newton was a fighter. He lived for a year, then two, then three. That's when his mother deserted him. Hannah married Barnabas Smith, a Church of England clergyman who lived in a nearby village. The prosperous sixty-three-year-old Reverend Smith would not allow little Isaac in his home—this was actually part of the marriage agreement. So off Hannah went.

Little Isaac was left in the care of his elderly grandparents. For eight years. Although his mother lived only a mile away, it might as well have been across an ocean. "A wife that expects to have a good name is always at home, as if she were lame," according to a book of English proverbs of the time. So Isaac probably rarely saw his mother.

Newton did discover that if he climbed a certain tree, he could see the steeple of the Anglican church where his stepfather preached.

Was Isaac at least close to his grandparents? No. He never wrote with any affection of his grandmother, not even noting it when she died. He *never* mentioned his grandfather in later life. When he was ten, his grandfather died and left Isaac absolutely nothing in his will. But during a time when most people remained illiterate, his grandmother did make sure Isaac learned the alphabet and the Bible.

Though many relatives lived close by, Newton seems not to have formed a bond with any of them. The only exception might have been his uncle, Hannah's brother William. Also a respectable Anglican clergyman, he was one of the few people in the family with education. William had a degree from Cambridge University, one of the oldest universities in the world.

The setting for Newton's lonely childhood was Woolsthorpe Manor, a gray limestone farmhouse with a stone barn attached. It was a working farm, set into a hill near a river, in Lincolnshire, in eastern England. The farm grew oats, corn, and barley. An orchard—home to the world's most famous apple tree—supplied snacks. Fences corralled over two hundred sheep and some forty cattle, considerably more than what neighbors had.

Although Isaac's father couldn't read or even sign his own name, Newton's family wasn't poor. They were prospering, not declining. They weren't servants; they *had* servants. Wool was the major source of income, plus rent from tenants who lived in cottages on the property and worked the land.

Newton would have inhaled the smell of manure every time he took a breath. The two-story house was run-down, with bare wooden floors. There were few books, no clock, no machines of any kind. The air would have been dusty, especially during sheep-shearing time.

The house was about a mile from the nearest major road, and it took a long time for any news to reach there. There were no newspapers yet to report all that was happening in London, a bursting-at-the-seams city of 400,000 people, 150 miles away.

It was a strange time of unrest and catastrophic events. Although the Church of England, the Anglican Church, was the state religion, there were those who saw it as corrupt and wanted to "purify" it. These Puritans challenged the very power of the king, the official head of the Church. Civil war broke out the same year Isaac was born. In 1649, King Charles I was beheaded and a new kingless government was installed. It lasted only eleven years before the dead king's son, Charles II, came to power. Some Puritans had already fled

England, establishing colonies in America.

Meanwhile, at Woolsthorpe, all was utterly quiet except for the moans of animals. The hills gently rolled through lush green valleys with dark, rich soil. The biggest excitement was the windmills that were beginning to replace water mills to grind the corn.

When Newton was eleven, his hated stepfather, the reverend, died. Now Hannah was a wealthy widow, with an income comparable to that of a noble-woman. She returned to Woolsthorpe Manor with three half-siblings for Newton. He hated them. But she also brought Smith's collection of books, some two to three hundred, mostly religious texts. Newton was an intensely religious boy and built shelves for the precious volumes—he was handy with wood. He also inherited a notebook of a thousand pages, still mostly blank, which to him was a treasure. Paper was expensive.

Newton was a loyal son, but he obviously nursed bitterness toward his mother and his now-dead step-father. A few years later, making a list of all his past sins, he included "Threatening my father and mother Smith to burn them and the house over them."

Most historians suspect that Newton's childhood of isolation and abandonment damaged him emotionally. It may have helped him as a scientist, though. Later in life he said that discovery was "the offspring of silence and meditation." From childhood on, much of his time was spent silent and alone. Thinking. Always thinking.

CHAPTER TWO

The Most Amazing Toys

*A*T AROUND AGE twelve, Newton was sent seven miles away to the King Edward Grammar School in Grantham, a village of a few hundred families. He boarded with the apothecary William Clark, who mixed medicines for folks in the village.

The druggist's workshop was probably the most stimulating place Newton had ever been. Medicine at the time was starting to develop new ideas about the nature of disease and medication. But druggists still also prescribed folk remedies: Some called for smoked horse testicles, spiders wrapped in silk, or dew collected in May. One potion was "300 millipedes well beaten (with their heads pulled off) suspended in four gallons of ale." There were people who believed that if you wrote "abracadabra" or drew signs of the zodiac on a piece of paper and kept it in your pocket, you would be protected from dreaded diseases such as the plague.

From Clark, Newton learned about herbs. He boiled leaves, seeds, and roots, and dried them in the sun, ground them with mortar and pestle, then formed them into pellets. This was probably Newton's first push into science. Also, Clark's brother had been a scholar at Cambridge University, and Newton was allowed free run of his bookshelves. This was his first exposure to the seventeenth-century Italian astronomer Galileo and other giants of science he would soon come to know better.

Clark had two stepsons, with whom Newton (surprise) did not get along. He was smart and probably not very tolerant of people who weren't. Clark also had a stepdaughter. Seventy years later, Catherine remembered holding hands with Newton. If this is true, it is the only evidence of any romantic attachment to a girl he ever showed. Newton had little use for women. He no doubt shared the long-held view that women were inferior—a "fair defect of Nature," as John Milton, the greatest poet of Newton's age, described them in *Paradise Lost*.

In Grantham he got the standard education of the day along with some eighty other boys. (The school was for boys only; most girls received whatever education they had at home.) Henry Stokes, the schoolmaster, drilled his students in Latin, some Greek and Hebrew, some arithmetic that was practical for farmers. Bible studies were the most important part of the curriculum in England. No natural philosophy (science). There were no encyclopedias, no dictionaries like the ones we have today. For that matter, English still had no hard-and-fast rules about basic spelling.

Oddly enough, Newton was placed in the bottom of his class at Grantham. Small for his age, he was a poor student at first, always lagging behind, labeled "inattentive" and "idle" in school reports.

He mostly kept to himself, and when he did mingle, it was nearly always with Catherine and her friends. The boys seemed resentful of him. Perhaps they made fun of his small size. Newton's feeble attempts to make them like him only backfired.

People who knew him from his school days remembered him as a "sober, silent, thinking lad." But they also recalled something else—"his strange inventions and extraordinary inclination for mechanical works." For Newton had a whole other side to him.

Skilled with his hands, he crafted wooden models of churches and other buildings. Any time he had money, he bought woodworking tools. With those tools, he made other tools. He carved "Isaac Newton" into every bench he ever sat on at school. Some of his creations were almost like toys. He constructed dollhouse furniture out of wood for Catherine and other girls. He invented a little four-wheeled vehicle for himself. While sitting in it, he could turn a crank to make it run.

Sometimes, unsuspecting farmers having their beers on market days would look up and see ill omens "from beyond" in the darkening sky—kites Newton created, with real lanterns attached to the tails.

Newton wasn't really the playful type, and with his toys, he was not so much playing as experimenting. When he made kites, for example, he was trying to figure out what shape, what proportions flew best.

He was learning the importance of measuring, testing, revising his ideas.

One of his most marvelous creations was a minia-ture windmill. Grantham was getting its first wind-powered mill, and every day he hung around and watched carpenters building it. How elegant this was—harnessing the power of the wind to do hard work like grinding corn. From his powers of observa-tion and ingenious imagination, Newton made his own wooden mill. Besides using wind to turn the cloth sails, he also constructed a tiny treadmill with a real live mouse to run it. When he tugged on a string tied to the mouse's tail, he produced "mouse-power."

One day, probably in a church, Newton saw something amazing—a new pendulum clock. He fell in love with measuring time. Sundials, or shadow-clocks, fascinated him—shadows moving regularly across a surface to indicate the time of day. He drew crude circles and arcs on walls, hammering in wooden pegs. He tied balls with strings to the pegs to meas-ure the shadows. And thus he tracked the sun's motion across the sky, day after day. If someone asked him what time it was, he could tell it to the nearest quarter hour, just by the shadows.

He kept an almanac charting the sun and the days of the month, and was able to compute a sun-calendar for the next twenty-eight years. This was at a time when the calendar was a matter of debate—England was isolated in using a calendar ten days out of step with the rest of Europe. Later Newton would urge reform of England's calendar.

A book called *The Mysteries of Nature and Art* by John Bate excited him. He faithfully copied passages and carried out projects in it. He followed recipes to make salves and to concoct inks in dozens of different colors. He taught himself about catching birds, melting metal, making fireworks, and how to draw. He left behind elaborate charcoal drawings of geometric shapes—as well as ships, birds, beasts, men, and plants.

He later claimed to have done his first "experiment" at age sixteen, though what it proved, if anything, is unclear. During a violent storm, he jumped against the wind, and then with it. He compared the length of these jumps with jumps he made on a windless day. The different measurements told him something (vague) about the strength of that particular storm. He boasted about his discovery to his classmates. They were underwhelmed.

Nor did Isaac's mother encourage his pursuits. Hannah did not see the point in educating Newton. Sometimes she actually pulled him out of school to help with farm chores back at Woolsthorpe. After all, his life's path was to manage the farm.

Legends about how uninterested he was in farming abound. While he was supposed to be tending the sheep, he would be experimenting with sheep's blood to make inks (his favorite color was always red). Rather than plowing fields, he'd be gathering and drying herbs and berries to make potions. Sent to fetch water, he'd spend hours observing how the water flowed in a stream, or building miniature waterwheels. He'd hide out in the hayloft, reading, when he should have been selling wool in the market.

It was his uncle William who rescued Isaac, making sure he went back to school. He may have realized Isaac was one of those rare boys capable of a university education. Back in Grantham again, Newton moved in with the school's headmaster, Mr. Stokes.

Around this time, there is a strange story of a bully kicking Newton in the stomach. Newton challenged the boy to a fight after class. It took place across the street from school. No one would have predicted it, but the smaller boy—Isaac—won. He not only beat up his opponent, but he pulled him along by the ears and pushed his face into a wall. Other boys were astounded by his show of force. It was a turning point for Isaac. After this, his behavior in the class-room completely changed. Before the fight, he was next to the bottom of the class. After, he rose to his rightful place. He was the top student at school.

But when he turned seventeen, Newton's mother again called him home. This time she enlisted a trusted servant to teach him about running the farm. It didn't work. Isaac made everyone laugh by leading a bridle to the barn, unaware that his horse was no longer attached to it. Fences he was in charge of mending were always falling down. He could not keep his eyes on the sheep, and they trampled the neighbor's corn, incurring fines for his mother to pay. On market days, he would bribe the servant to drop him off outside of town with his books and gadgets. Nine miserable months dragged by.

His uncle William stepped in again. He and the Grantham headmaster together urged Hannah to send Isaac back to school. When Mr. Stokes offered to drop the fee, she finally relented. Isaac returned to Grantham in 1660 for the last bit of education necessary to prepare for the university. The servants at Woolsthorpe, who found him both lazy and foolish, positively rejoiced to see him go.

On the day Newton finally graduated from grammar school, Mr. Stokes gave a speech in his honor. He reportedly had tears of pride in his eyes, urging the other boys to be more like Isaac. It was said that they had tears in their eyes, too—tears of relief, perhaps, at seeing the last of their unpopular classmate.

CHAPTER THREE

Learning Outside Class

*I*N 1661, NEWTON left the stifling rural life behind. Cambridge University was a hundred miles—a three-day carriage ride—to the south. Cambridge was Newton's new home, and it was obviously congenial to him. He planted himself there like an apple tree ready to flourish, and stayed, more or less, for nearly thirty-five years.

Cambridge was actually a collection of colleges, then numbering sixteen. The College of the Holy and Undivided Trinity was the largest and best funded. Trinity College, as it was called, was Newton's. It had tennis courts, stables, formal gardens with fountains, a library, a chapel. Visitors today can still see the ground-floor rooms Newton had as a lowly first-year student. A grand dining hall was dominated by a huge portrait of King Henry VIII (of six-wives fame), founder of Trinity. It was Henry who had created the Church of England because the pope would not grant him a divorce.

To Newton, stepping onto the splendid campus might have been the thrill that entering Hogwarts School was to the young Harry Potter. The great majority of people in England were like most of Newton's family—farmers with no education. Here he encountered England's elite—the sons of nobility and wealthy landowners. Many illustrious men in English history were Trinity alumni. (Women were not allowed to earn degrees at Cambridge until 1947.) Newton was smaller, older, odder—but smarter—than most of his classmates.

Newton's mother apparently still opposed his education. A wealthy widow, she was unwilling to pay for it. So he entered Trinity as a subsizar. Subsizars were poor students who earned their keep by performing menial tasks for their wealthier classmates. Newton, the smartest guy around, had to clean others' rooms, even emptying their chamber pots. He would serve bread and beer at the dining tables, then eat what remained after the other students left.

Being at the very bottom of the Cambridge social ladder must have been humiliating. Acquiring money became Newton's primary concern. He realized early on that he could earn a little extra by lending it and charging interest. He kept careful records of his small money-lending operation.

He also kept a meticulous notebook of his expenses. His very first purchase was a lock for his desk. He noted a few frivolous purchases (cherries, a tart, a chess board, a little wine, the occasional bottle of beer), but most expenses were practical (a pound of candles, paper, ink, a chamber pot, two spoons, socks). Of the first ten books he bought, six were on history and mathematics, and four were on religious subjects.

By this time, the king and the Anglican Church were again in control of England. The Church, with patrons among the nobility and in Parliament, controlled the course of study and professorships at Cambridge. The university prepared students to become either clergymen or doctors, or to stay on at Cambridge as fellows and pursue a life of learning.

All fellows at Cambridge were required to swear to the beliefs of the Anglican Church.

Newton took religion very seriously. We don't know what inspired it, but at age nineteen, Newton apparently underwent some sort of religious crisis. He drew up a list of all the sins he could remember having committed so far. His list of sins numbered fifty-eight.

Some were serious—such as the threat to burn down his parents' house with them in it. He also wrote of "wishing death" to others, "striking many," "punching my sister," "falling out with the servants," the beating up of another boy, and many occasions of "peevishness."

Among his lesser misdemeanors, he listed having unclean thoughts and neglecting to pray. He stole cherry dumplings, called people names, and did forbidden things on Sundays, like making a mousetrap.

He seemed to carry a huge burden of guilt. It's hard to say whom he disapproved of more—himself or others. Certainly the rowdy antics of other students disturbed him. Always something of a prig, he wrote an entire letter to one classmate begging him to repent for drinking too much.

Prigs usually aren't popular, and Newton was probably the butt of many jokes. Completely unathletic, he didn't play tennis or the other sports that forged bonds among students. He tried gambling and card games, but guilt at such sinfulness made him stop. Mostly he was invisible, never part of the college community. Perhaps he was frustrated that humans weren't as orderly and predictable as clocks. He didn't get along with his first roommate, enduring (or inflicting) eighteen months of tension.

Then John Wickins, a year younger than Isaac, arrived at Cambridge. He didn't like his roommate either, and one day ran into Newton while both were out walking. The two unhappy students "agreed to shake off their present disorderly companions and chum together," according to Wickins. He became Newton's roommate—for the next twenty years—and his only friend. We know little about Wickins, except that he worked as Newton's assistant until a mysterious parting, after which they never spoke to each other again.

Now, what did Newton study? Classes at Cambridge had changed little over the previous four hundred years. The curriculum covered Homer and

Virgil and other ancient Greek and Latin poets, lots of Biblical studies, logic, and languages—Greek, Latin, and Hebrew.

The intellectual atmosphere was stale and sleepy, especially compared to other universities around Europe. Many different branches of science—even math and astronomy—were lumped together under "philosophy." The works of the ancient Greeks such as Plato and his pupil Aristotle were used to teach students about logic and rhetoric. Aristotle, who lived in the fourth century B.C., used a set of assumptions to arrive logically at a conclusion. For example, "All men are mortal; no gods are mortal; therefore no men are gods."

Aristotle taught that beautiful concepts were more important than firsthand experience, knowledge arrived at through experiments. For example, Aristotle said that objects of different weights fall at different speeds—meaning that something heavy will fall faster than something of lighter weight and will hit the ground first. This sounds logical; it seems to make sense—and Aristotle saw no need to test the concept. Aristotelian philosophy rested on a lot of talk or argument. The joke was that some scholars would spend hours discussing how many teeth a horse had without actually bothering to look in a horse's mouth. Measuring, quantifying, numbering. What use was that?

According to Aristotle, only four elements made up everything in the world—Fire, Air, Water, Earth. And the earth was the center of the universe, the other planets and the sun revolving around it.

As a student at Cambridge, Newton somehow never seemed to finish the required reading. He ignored the tutor, a professor of Greek, who was assigned to him. No one cared. As long as he wasn't speaking out against the Anglican Church, he had considerable freedom. So he turned his back on the traditional curriculum and got himself to the library. There he threw himself into private research inspired by writers a little more current than Aristotle.

Who were they?

One was Nicolaus Copernicus, the Polish astronomer who had died in 1543. Newton devoured his book *On the Revolutions of the Celestial Spheres*, which traced the movements of the planets. In a revolutionary theory for his day, Copernicus said that Earth and other planets revolved around the sun. For this and other ideas he is considered the father of modern astronomy.

Galileo Galilei, who died the year Newton was born, was a mathematics lecturer at universities in Italy, where he built on Copernicus's work in astronomy. (Toward the end of his life, the Catholic Church put Galileo under house arrest for supporting Copernicus's views.) Galileo was the first to use a telescope to scan the heavens, and it was Galileo who invented the pendulum clock that so fascinated Newton. His inspiration was a huge lamp swinging from a church ceiling. He used the beat of his own pulse and timed the swings—although the distance covered by the swings became shorter and shorter, they still took the same amount of time as longer swings.

Galileo also was among the first to conduct experiments, although he didn't deem them essential in the way Newton would later. In one experiment, Galileo dropped various weights from the top of the famous Leaning Tower of Pisa. Was Aristotle's theory right? Would heavier weights fall faster and hit the ground first? From the Tower of Pisa, the weights fell at the same speed. In other words, Aristotle was wrong.

Newton kept on reading. He studied the work of Johannes Kepler, a German astronomer who had died in 1630. Like Copernicus, Kepler also believed that the planets traveled around the sun. But Copernicus assumed the paths were perfect circles. Kepler realized that each orbital path was an ellipse, a flattened oval. This became the first of Kepler's three laws of planetary motion. His second law was that the speed at which a planet travels changes depending on its distance from the sun. And third, there is a specific mathematical relationship between a planet's distance from the sun and the time it takes a planet to orbit the sun.

Newton inhaled the work of René Descartes, a French mathematician who had died in 1650. Descartes questioned everything. The only thing he said he was absolutely sure of was his own existence: "I think, therefore I am," he wrote. Today we consider Descartes the father of modern philosophy.

Newton painstakingly tackled *Discourse on Method*, the difficult masterpiece by Descartes. It came up with a whole new kind of math—analytical geometry—which dealt with abstract reasoning. Newton would read two or three pages, go back and reread them, and only when he was sure of their meaning would he proceed to the next couple of pages.

Newton found an English philosopher, Francis Bacon (also a Trinity alumnus), especially stimulating. Bacon's *Novum Organum* (New Methodology) was exhilarating—"Knowledge is power," he had written. To Newton, Bacon was the very model of a natural philosopher, way ahead of his time (he died in 1626), promoting practical experiment as a way to test theo-ries. Bacon attempted to sum up the varied roles that one crucial missing word —*scientist*—would someday encompass: "The study of nature . . . is engaged in by the mechanic, the mathematician, the physician, the alchemist . . ." It was the best definition thus far of what Newton wanted to be.

As for classes at Cambridge, Newton probably attended the lectures given by Isaac Barrow at Trinity. In 1664, Barrow became the first professor of mathematics at the university. (There were no profes-sors of chemistry or astronomy until the next centu-ry.) Barrow's official title was Lucasian Professor of Mathematics—the same position now held by physi-cist Stephen Hawking.

Newton's interest in mathematics, especially the mathematics of moving objects, really took off once he encountered Barrow. The closest thing Newton had to a mentor at Trinity, Barrow found him boggling and unpromising at first. But after a few years he bragged about his protégé: "Very young . . . but of an extraordinary genius and proficiency."

The young scholar bought an astrology book at the Stourbridge Fair near Cambridge, the annual mar-ket for buying and selling wool, silk, books, toys. Astrology is the study of how the locations of the stars and planets influence people's lives. Considered a legitimate scientific study then, astrology involved complex math. When Newton discovered that he could not understand the book because he lacked knowledge of geometry and trigonometry, he decided to read *Elements*, Barrow's edition of the ancient Greek Euclid's work on geometry.

Newton started asking himself questions—about the nature of matter, cosmic order, light, colors, and sensations. The world of the 1660s was changing dra-matically—new discoveries of stars (which Newton followed closely), new knowledge about the earth's geography (witness the American colonies in "New" England), new technology (like the pendulum clocks that so mesmerized him).

In his second year, Newton began to fill up a notebook with a series of wide-ranging scientific entries. He called the book *Quaestiones Quaedam Philosophicae* (Certain Philosophical Questions). He began boldly, with a Latin statement meaning "Plato is my friend, Aristotle is my friend, but my best friend is truth." He was announcing that he was an independent thinker. And—like Leonardo da Vinci two hundred years before him—he wanted to think about *everything*.

This notebook was the birth of Newton the scientist. All in his tiny, meticulous handwriting, in faded ink, he listed forty-five topics he wanted to research. The list shows how encyclopedic his interests were—time, eternity, space, motion, stars, planets, light, vision, colors, sounds, smells. There were no real encyclopedias yet—Newton was creating one for himself. One topic suggested others—also on the list were memory, imagination, sleep, dreams, and God. His attitude was one of constant questioning, never taking a so-called expert's word for anything. If something happened in the natural world, it happened for a reason—he intended to search for causes and effects.

The notebook shows Newton's use of controlled experiments, a method favored, most notably, by Francis Bacon before him. (In a controlled experiment, all variables remain the same except for the one being tested.) Newton at first had no money for equipment. So he used himself—and some of his earliest experiments sound insane. To test theories about light and vision, for example, he decided to use his own eyeballs.

He began simply, harmlessly. At sunset, he would take a dark feather and place it in front of his eye in such a way that light produced "glorious colors," noting the fringe of colors around the blackness of the feather.

Then he wanted to see what happened to vision by staring at the sun. Would the colors look different? So he stared at the sun with one eye until he could bear it no longer. Yes, all the colors changed. But he didn't seem to realize that staring at the sun was harmful, even when blobs of color floated before his eyes for days afterward. After one of his experiments, he had to lie in bed in a dark room for two weeks before normal vision returned.

Newton also actually stuck things in his eye—a finger, a bodkin (a long needle with a flat tip used to sew leather), and other sharp objects. He poked underneath his eyeball, almost to the back of the eye socket, to see what colors or changes in vision the pressure produced. White and colored circles appeared and faded. What did this prove? Probably nothing. But he wrote every experiment down, step by step. Readers of his notebook continue to marvel · that he didn't blind himself.

Heading into his third year at Cambridge, Newton surrendered himself to study. He would start to get out of bed in the morning and then sit for hours, reading or just lost in contemplation. Or he'd forget about sleep altogether, staying up all night. He also forgot to eat. It was said that Newton had a cat that grew notoriously fat from eating all the untouched food on his plate. Presumably Newton grew thinner.

It was not a healthy or well-rounded life.

Despite his terrible attendance in class, Newton went on to earn his bachelor's degree in January 1665. He assumed he was on his way to a secure academic future. At a later date he would be required to take holy orders and become an Anglican clergyman, but for now his solitary life of the mind continued.

Charting the night skies, for example, was among his cherished studies, a part of his routine ever since he had listed "Of the sun, stars and planets and comets" as a heading in his notebook. Around this time he observed a new comet shooting fire toward the west, low on the horizon. Happily, night after night, he stayed outdoors tracking the path of the comet as it moved against the pattern of the fixed stars.

A comet, superstitious people believed, was a portent of an evil event. And what happened that fall, they believed, proved it.

The bubonic plague struck England—with a vengeance.

CHAPTER FOUR

The Apple

HE BUBONIC PLAGUE, or Black Death, was a disgusting, painful, highly contagious disease. Periodically it would sweep through countries, killing millions. In the outbreak of 1348, the plague had killed one of every four people in Europe. Early symptoms were flulike—fever, aches—followed by the telltale sign: ugly black swellings in the armpits. Death usually came in a few days.

In 1665, there hadn't been much progress in ending the plague, or even discovering its cause: probably fleas spread the disease from rats to humans. And the streets in the bulging city of London—crowded and filthy, with wooden houses built practically on top of each other—turned out to be a perfect breeding ground for rats. Suddenly Londoners were falling ill by the thousands.

With no cure for the plague, the only way to remain healthy was to avoid contamination. People tried to flee from other people and get out to the countryside. Those who fell sick were confined to their houses, the doors marked with large red crosses. Officials would hand them food through the windows.

Public places like Cambridge University shut down; everyone was sent home. Most students tried to continue their studies by moving to nearby villages with their tutors.

Newton hadn't relied on a tutor in years. There was no place for him to go but back to Woolsthorpe Manor. His stay was to last eighteen months. During this time, one of every six Londoners died of the plague.

Many people interpreted the catastrophic year as either the work of the devil or as punishment from God. Isaac Newton, however, came to consider it the most miraculous year of his life.

Back at Woolsthorpe and absolved of farm duties, he set up a study in his upstairs bedroom, closed the shutters, and carved out for himself a space of peace and quiet. He kept bread and water in his room, some' times indulging in wine. He concocted and regularly took a potion he thought would protect him from plague and smallpox—olive oil, rosewater, beeswax, wine, and turpentine. He went for long, silent walks, or sometimes sat in the garden contemplating the apple trees. There was nothing to do but think.

He took the thousand-page notebook he'd inherited from his stepfather, and named it his "Waste Book"— a term meaning a practical journal. It was his store' room for great thoughts. Forever methodical, he labeled one section "Problems" and quickly came up with twenty-two questions he wanted to answer about lines and curves. This was to be his self-study program during his forced "vacation."

He continued with his reading of a stimulating book by Galileo called *Dialogue Concerning the Two Chief World Systems*. This was the book in which Galileo talked about how objects fall to the earth. From studying Kepler, Newton had already begun thinking about orbital paths. Newton puzzled over whether these two things were linked. Could the force at work on planets in outer space be the same force that made objects fall to the ground? If so, what type of force could this be?

Thinking, always thinking, Newton made the connection.

There is a famous legend about Newton and an apple. (On four separate occasions later in his life, Newton claimed the story was true.) In 1666, while he was napping under an apple tree in the orchard at Woolsthorpe, an apple fell on his head. He awoke with a jolt. Why did an apple always fall down? he wondered. Why not sideways, or even up? Suddenly he began thinking that if the force that made the apple fall to the ground extended to the height of the tree, then it could also extend all the way out into space; he understood that the apple falling and the moon orbiting were governed by the same force: gravity—or what Newton referred to as the Law of Universal Gravitation.

While it is true that Woolsthorpe had apple trees, the apple story is misleading. It implies a magical moment when *all is revealed*. A more accurate version of the story would be that, for Newton, every idea, even a brilliant one, was a process. When asked later in life how he went about solving a problem, he said, "By thinking on it continually." He went on to elabo-rate. "I keep the subject constantly before me, and wait till the first dawnings open slowly, by little and

little, into a full and clear light." Insights didn't come to him in a flash, out of nowhere, but instead with numerous hesitations. He made mistakes but he was patient in finding and correcting them. Losing his focus was never a problem.

As if gravity wasn't enough to tax his brain with, Newton worked on many of his other twenty-two "problems" at the same time. For example, using algebra, he came up with a method to find the area under almost every algebraic curve then known.

Then, in his spare time, he worked on another problem: Algebra could find the value of "x," where "x" is a single unknown number. But how can you find the value of an unknown number that keeps changing? Newton came up with a way of calculating rate of change. He referred to the changing (or flow-ing) quantity as a "fluent" and to its rate of change as a "fluxion." He called his new invention his "method of fluxions." He even developed a system of symbols to use—clumsy ones, but they worked.

No one was aware of it yet, but he had just invented calculus, a mathematical method of describ-ing how things change over time. Take, for example, a ball tossed into the air. Using calculus, you can describe the path of the ball, even though the speed and direction of the ball are constantly changing. Calculus was the vital tool Newton would need for the rest of his life's work.

He also began to study optics, to investigate the nature of light. How did it travel? What was it com-posed of? Was light white as everyone since Aristotle had believed? (Wrong.) Were colors merely a mixture of white light and different degrees of darkness? (Wrong again.)

At the Stourbridge Fair, Newton bought a glass prism, a child's toy believed to *create* bright colors when light passed through it. Upstairs in his dark-ened Woolsthorpe room, Newton began ingenious experiments with prisms to prove that light *contained* all the different colors.

First, he passed a beam of sunlight through the prism and observed, on a wall twenty-two feet from the window, that the white light split into separate bands of color. To prove that the light itself—and not a trick of the prism—contained all the colors, he went a crucial step further. This time he threw light that passed through the prism onto a piece of wood that had a hole punched in it so that only one band of color—say green—passed through the hole. Then he put a *second* prism in the path of the green light. Was the prism coloring the light? If so, Newton reasoned, then the green would change and be separated into bands of colors again. But the green band of light remained green. The prism had no effect on it. Since the prism was not coloring the light, white light must contain the colors in it. Aristotle was wrong. Newton was right.

Sunlight may *appear* white. But Newton proved that white light is made up of colors mixed together: violet, indigo, blue, green, yellow, orange, and red. (Black is the absence of light.) What the prism did was separate white light into the different colors of light. Thus, Newton was the first person to really understand the rainbow.

Carefully documented, these would become the most famous optical experiments in the history of science. And this time he had learned how to test his optical theories without poking his eyes out.

His patience and concentration were unparalleled—perhaps no one else in history has ever had the same power to focus, like a sharp beam of light. And at Woolsthorpe there were no interruptions. He might not have been so ready to break new ground had he remained ensconced at Cambridge. Here, no one bothered him. Every day was the same. He had no other responsibilities.

Those who made predictions from numbers had warned that 1666 was going to be apocalyptic—the "Year of the Beast." And indeed the plague had been followed by a huge fire in London, spreading chaos throughout the city.

Newton's followers, instead, called this plague year his *annus mirabilis*—the wondrous year. It couldn't have been more intellectually rich. With no help other than books and tools like the prism that he found on his own, he laid the foundations for his life's work in motion, mathematics, and optics. He was discovering the laws by which nature operated.

For the time being, only one person appreciated the immensity of his achievement. Himself. "I was in the prime of my age for invention," he said later, in one of the biggest understatements ever made.

He was only twenty-four.

CHAPTER FIVE

Newton versus Hooke

*A*FTER ENOUGH TIME passed with no new cases of plague, Cambridge and other public places reopened. Newton was able to return to his sanctuary, the university.

In 1667, he became a fellow at Trinity College—a scholar who was paid to live at the university pursuing a life of the mind. Becoming a fellow was trickier than it sounds. There were four intense days of oral examination based on the university curriculum, the one Newton had basically ignored. Still, he pulled it off and immediately purchased twelve yards of fabric for a scholar's gown.

Now he had freedom to continue his studies, with little asked in return. Fellows had to take a vow of celibacy (not a problem for Newton), and to promise to take holy orders within seven years of receiving their master's degree. They also had to take an oath swearing to the official beliefs of the Church of England, including the doctrine of the Holy Trinity, which states that God manifests himself as Father, Son, and Holy Spirit.

As devout a Christian as he was, Newton wouldn't be Newton if he hadn't questioned Church doctrines. He believed that only God the Father was divine. What? A fellow at Trinity College not believing in the Trinity? Cambridge University was tolerant of just about anything in its fellows, but not heresy. Newton signed the oath and kept his beliefs to himself.

He was allowed to dine at the fellows' table, although mealtime, as usual, was not the high point of his day. Other fellows later described him sitting at the table and forgetting to take porridge, only remembering that he was there to eat after the table had been cleared. He never started up a conversation, or joined others'.

His careful notebook of expenses during this time

shows a flurry of splurges. In addition to buying a tablecloth and six napkins and a new bed, he made several visits to taverns and played a little cards (always losing). He chose some new furniture and curtains—all crimson.

Then it seems as if Newton got out his books and shut the door. He visited no one. Sometimes, when guests paid the occasional visit, he would go off to get a bottle of wine from his study, sit down at his desk, and forget company was there. Hours later his visitors would finally creep out without disturbing him.

One of them once told a risqué story about a nun in Newton's presence, and Newton immediately broke off the relationship.

Unlike many young scholars, Newton made no grand tours of Europe. Outwardly, in fact, his life changed very little. Newton was, above all else, "studious"—always with a book before him, a pen in hand. There was to be no marriage, no children, not much to gossip about. He would never travel except to London, fifty miles south of Cambridge and the only big city in England. His journeys were all in the land of his own imagination, an imagination without boundaries.

But it was not a life without drama. There was the drama of discovery. Less nobly, there were his long-running feuds with other scientists.

In 1669, Newton's math professor, Isaac Barrow, resigned. (He later became chaplain to King Charles II.) Barrow suggested that his eccentric pupil succeed him. So it was, that at twenty-seven, his hair already turning silver, Isaac Newton became the new Lucasian Professor of Mathematics. It was quite a feat—one that made him known to famous men outside Cambridge.

This prestigious job gave him lodging, a small salary, and even more freedom. He only had to give one lecture a week to students. He was to speak on geometry, astronomy, optics, or some other discipline, then deposit a copy of the lecture in the library.

For the subject of his first lectures, he chose optics. He set out his then-radical view on the nature of light and colors.

Newton's lectures failed to mesmerize. He stared into space, pausing at length between sentences. Sometimes he had no audience at all. People snickered that poor Newton, in his scarlet professor's gown, went on reading his speech anyway—addressing the walls. In fairness to Newton, empty halls were not uncommon. The wealthy playboys attending Trinity College at Cambridge had many other diversions and weren't interested in science. Newton made no effort to simplify his ideas; his students had no understanding of their importance. They saw him as an unusually young, unusually peculiar professor.

The teaching requirement was apparently not even enforced. Newton may have put his lectures in the library without ever delivering them. As usual, no one at Cambridge complained.

The new Dr. Newton was the stereotypical absentminded professor holed up in his "ivory tower." (Actually his rooms were usually on the first floor, with a garden and shed.) He was careless with clothes (he slept in them) and left his hair uncombed. Alone in his stuffy rooms, he could still tell time by the shadows on the wall. He did enjoy a stroll around his garden, but it drove him crazy to see a weed in it. Not one to do the work himself, he hired a gardener.

He worked on his many projects until two or three o'clock every night, so he usually missed morning chapel. Sometimes he skipped evening chapel, too. He did attend on Sundays. Otherwise, he seemed to begrudge time spent eating or sleeping or doing any other human activity. He was odd but nevertheless held in some awe. When he drew diagrams with his stick on freshly laid gravel, no one would dare disturb the diagrams until the next rain washed them away. Students even today speak of the cloisters by the quadrangle where Newton is said to have measured the speed of sound by stamping his feet and timing the arrival of the echo.

In his chambers, Newton continued his work. For studying the planets, he needed something new in the way of a telescope. Large, bulky telescopes had been around since Galileo's time, but objects seen through the lenses appeared distorted, with fringes of color at their edges. People had been trying for years to design a better model. With his own hands, Newton set about constructing a functioning reflecting telescope, one that used a mirror instead of a lens. Scottish mathematician James Gregory had made designs for one in 1663, but Newton was the first to actually build one. He cast the mirror himself, grinding and polishing it. About six inches long, Newton's telescope magnified objects about forty times and gave a sharper image than was possible with a large lens.

Newton was eager to show off his extremely cool new toy to the members of the Royal Society in London. In 1672, after he sent them one, they promptly elected him a member.

Founded only twelve years earlier, the Royal Society was like a science club for wealthy men. Intended for "the improving of natural knowledge by experiment," this was the official association of gentlemen philosophers. There were no professional scientists as there are today.

This was an age of brilliant men in London, a city that was reinventing itself. In 1666, the city, constructed mostly of wood and straw, had caught fire. Fires were all too common, but this one had jumped completely out of control, from one thatched roof to another. The Great Fire of London raged for four dry, windy days and nights, spreading in all directions. It devastated the city, leaving many hundreds of thousands homeless. London had to be rebuilt—out of stone, not wood.

Many of the men involved in the rebuilding of London were already part of the Royal Society. There was Christopher Wren, a famous astronomer and an even more famous architect; Edmond Halley, whose exciting research on comets later led to one being named for him (it is next expected to return in 2061); Samuel Pepys, whose diary gives a vivid picture of the times; and Robert Hooke, the author and illustra' tor of *Micrographia*, a fascinating volume with engravings of natural phenomena as viewed under the new microscope. A man of too many accomplishments to count, Hooke also designed the rebuilt Bethlehem Hospital, or "Bedlam," London's first modern hospi' tal for the mentally ill.

The Royal Society met monthly, often cantanker' ously—many members were prickly personalities who could hardly stand to be in same room. Yet it was crucial to science at the time, providing a place where smart men could exchange new ideas in person instead of writing letters. Its motto was "*Nullius in verba*" or "Take no one's word for it." Talk of religion or poli' tics was banned, lest the men do nothing but argue. The goal was to distance themselves from folklore, superstitions. But this was a transitional time for sci' ence. So in addition to readings of scholarly papers, popular topics at early meetings were "monstrosities" (a puppy born without a mouth, four conjoined pigs, a two'headed calf, werewolves). At one meeting, the men watched a spider try to escape from "powder made from unicorn horn"; at another, they tried to prove spontaneous generation by making insects from cheese. But as the Society made progress, it left more time for published scientific papers to be read and less time for research involving unicorns.

Newton was to have a stormy relationship with the Society—no surprise there—although many years later it came under his control.

The idea of publishing his discoveries filled him with nameless dread. "I see not what there is desir- able in public esteem," he said. So celebrity was no lure, and he feared plagiarism if his ideas were made public. Above all, Newton couldn't abide the prospect of criticism. The easiest way to avoid it was to publish nothing.

But in 1672, after the excited response to his tele- scope, he got carried away and published his first sci- entific paper. It presented three prism experiments, carefully described so that others could repeat them. In detailing his discovery of the composite nature of white light, he explained how his experiments led him to devise the reflecting telescope.

With mixed feelings, Newton saw his piece published in the Royal Society's *Philosophical Transactions*, the first journal devoted to science. "Theory about Light and Colors" was the first article they published that used experiments to overturn an earlier accepted theory. In science, the word "theory" means much more than a guess or a hunch; it is a group of ideas that is based on observations and experiments and that explains why something happens. Single facts are only little tidbits of knowl-edge—they're not very enlightening on their own, but grouped together they may create theories.

Publishing his theory in the Society's journal and putting himself out there was a big risk for Newton. At first he breathed easy. His paper was generally well received by leaders of the scientific community. But not everyone applauded. The strongest criticism came from Robert Hooke, who was brilliant but a bit of a know-it-all. He explored a wide range of scientific subjects, many of which overlapped with Newton's own pursuits. Hooke inspired Newton when he wrote things like, "The science of nature has been already too long made only a work of the brain and the fancy. It is now high time that it should return to the plainness and soundness of observations." Hooke, too, conducted experiments using prisms to study light but reached different, contradictory conclusions. He, too, had worked out his own theory of colors.

At the Royal Society, Hooke was the first Curator of Experiments. He amazed members with demonstrations of vacuums, air pumps, magnets, and much else, including dissections of dogs. Hooke dabbled in everything, but his focus was "things of use"—improved chimneys, systems for carrying heavy weights up from mines, refining the process of glassmaking, softening steel. As many real accom-plishments as he had, Hooke did like to take credit where it wasn't necessarily due.

Two weeks after the publication of Newton's article on light, Hooke wrote a long critique. He objected to Newton's conviction that just a couple of experiments all by themselves were proof of Newton's theory of the nature of light. He called the theory a "hypothesis"—something yet to be proven.

To Newton, all this was "rudeness." The need to explain himself enraged him. But what really sent him into a fury was Hooke's condescending tone promot-ing his own contradictory ideas. (At least, that was how Newton interpreted it.)

All these years of no food and sleepless nights—and *this* was his thanks? Newton was unprepared for anything but total acceptance. He was right—period, end of sentence. Hooke's letter was his first encounter with the sharing-and-getting-feedback part of science. And Newton didn't like it.

His first response was to resign from the Royal Society, but members talked him out of it. He whined that he "had sacrificed [his] peace, a matter of real substance."

Then he began a lifelong vendetta against Hooke. He sat down to write a counterattack. Hooke had spent three or four hours writing his objections to

Newton's article. Newton spent three months on his reply.

In fact, Hooke *had* been one of his influences. But now he charged that Hooke's ideas were "not only *insufficient*, but in some respects *unintelligible.*"

Hooke made the mistake of writing back, and the more he wrote, the more enraged Newton became. He answered Hooke's objections carefully and, at first, patiently, but later with growing irritation. Newton typically made twenty or thirty drafts of a single document, using a quill pen to cover pages in his tiny spidery handwriting. Dealing with Hooke was taking up valuable time.

His fear of publicity grew worse. His only recourse, as he saw it, was to stop publishing his findings. "I see a man must either resolve to put out nothing new or to become a slave to defend it," he pouted.

Over the years, Newton's relations with Hooke deteriorated further. In a classic case of the pot calling the kettle black, he once accused Hooke of being "a man of strange unsociable temper."

Yet circumstances in the small world of English science demanded that the two men try to remain civil. They continued to exchange letters with a veneer of courtesy. But Newton turned away from the Royal Society, which he associated with Hooke. The quarrel was kept alive for thirty-one years. It ended only with the death of Robert Hooke.

Certainly one could say that Newton's reaction to criticism was childish, even irrational. It was also bad for science. Sharing ideas is a critical part of the scientific progress. But ever since he had spent so much time alone as a boy, Newton liked to spin in his own orbit. Now he went into genuine mourning over the loss of his "former serene liberty."

The result was that he failed to engage with other leading scientists, perhaps impeding his own and others' progress. He would not let others stand on his shoulders.

Most importantly, Newton delayed the publication of *Opticks*—the full account of his revolutionary theory of light and color—for some thirty years, all the way until 1704. The year was no coincidence—Hooke had died in 1703.

CHAPTER SIX

Math War

ODAY, ANYONE CAN learn calculus in an advanced high-school class or college course. In the seventeenth century, it didn't exist.

Calculus is the mathematics of change, solving problems such as those involving the acceleration of moving objects. With calculus you can accurately figure out the position of a planet in its orbit. It gives a more exact way to calculate areas, volumes, and other quantities than the ancient Greeks had been able to do using geometry. Today it is used in the work of space scientists, architectural engineers, and theoretical physicists.

In 1669, Newton gave his old professor Isaac Barrow a valuable manuscript. Written in Latin, it was known as *De Analysi per Aequationes Numero Terminorum Infinitas* (translated later as *On Analysis by Infinite Series*). This work contained many of Newton's conclusions about what he called his "fluxional method," which he had worked out during his "wondrous" year at Woolsthorpe. Barrow wanted to send the paper to a few colleagues in England and Europe. Newton agreed, very reluctantly. But *De Analysi* was not immediately published, thanks to Newton's then-policy of not going public with anything.

Seven years later, in 1676, a brilliant German mathematician named Gottfried Wilhelm Leibniz published his own version of calculus. He created a different system of symbols—easier, in fact, than Newton's.

So Leibniz published his work first, but Newton and his supporters claimed that Leibniz had seen *De Analysi* years earlier. That he had stolen Newton's work.

Thus began what is now known as the Calculus Priority Dispute. A math war over who got there first.

Newton wrote two long, furious letters to Leibniz. He was in a terrible bind, desperate to prove his earlier discovery of calculus but still not wanting to "share." So what Newton's letter did was explain calculus— but in code: "5accdae19effh11i413m9n6oqqr8s" and so forth. Leibniz could not understand what was written because Newton kept the key to the code. Later Newton made the correspondence public and seemed to think that doing so vindicated his position.

Newton was proving himself unfit for genuine scientific exchange, while at the same time, many were trying to engage him in just that. It was a stress-ful period. He may have suffered some sort of break-down. His mother also fell ill. They were still not especially close—he had visited her only a handful of times—but he dutifully nursed her during her final feverish days, until she died in 1679. Her sole heir, he took most of 1680 to put the family's affairs in order.

He withdrew further into his shell.

In 1684, Leibniz published a paper on calculus, without ever mentioning his rival. This infuriated Newton, but he took years to reply. In 1704, he pub-lished On the Quadrature of Curves, which laid out his calculus, using different symbols from Leibniz's to create equations.

Meanwhile he let his resentment fester into an open sore. In unrelated papers, he would suddenly break into a rant against Leibniz. To his enemy's face he was oily with false flattery. "I value friends more highly than mathematical discoveries," he once lied.

At any point the two men could have agreed to share credit on the principle that, as Leibniz once said, "One man makes one contribution, another man another."

"Second inventors count for nothing," was Newton's response.

Finally, in 1711, Leibniz appealed to the Royal Society to settle the dispute. Alas for Leibniz, Newton was active again in the Society. Actually, no one could have predicted it, but Newton in his old age had become president of the Society.

Mathematicians all over England and Europe took sides in the dispute, even though it took guts to go against Newton. It was the biggest controversy in the history of mathematics.

"Slimy" is one word for the way Newton used his position as president of the Royal Society to deal with Leibniz. In this capacity he appointed an "impartial" committee to decide whether he or Leibniz was the inventor of calculus. Newton packed the review

committee with his fans. The committee's 1713 judg-
ment favored—surprise—Newton. Anonymously, he
himself wrote the official report of the committee.
Then he wrote a favorable review of the report (again
anonymously) for the Royal Society's *Philosophical
Transactions.*

This fight—lasting thirty years—ended only
when Leibniz died in 1716, his reputation in shreds.
Newton got the news in a letter: "Mr. Leibniz is
dead; and the dispute is finished." Newton, still
bitter, bragged to others that he had broken
Leibniz's heart.

So who was right? Most scholars agree that
Newton *was* the first to invent calculus. But Leibniz,
working independently, was the first to *publish* his
findings. So phobic about publishing, Newton
believed that what counted was the work of invention, not when the world found out about it and
was able to put it to use.

However, mathematicians eventually adopted
Leibniz's easier symbols, a mathematical language that
has survived to the present day with few changes.
Newton's symbols were efficient for him, but not uni-
versally understandable.

The petty dispute between two gifted men harmed relations between the British scientific community and the rest of Europe. And English mathematicians, who had been the best in the world, wanted nothing to do with Leibniz's work. For fifty years they refused to use his calculus notation—and therefore couldn't communicate outside their own country.

Newton rigged the Calculus Priority Dispute and won, but at what cost?

CHAPTER SEVEN

Star War

*H*OWEVER TIME-CONSUMING the senseless feuding with Leibniz was, Newton also found the energy to carry on a twenty-year-long name-calling brawl with the leading astronomer of the day.

Mild-mannered John Flamsteed was England's first Astronomer Royal, head of the newly established Royal Greenwich Observatory. His job was to prepare charts of stars for the British Navy so ships wouldn't get lost—especially important now that travel to and from the new American colonies was increasing.

Using a telescope and sextant, Flamsteed worked every single night, noting more than a thousand observations a year. If you wanted to know anything about the skies, he was the man to ask. The only man.

In 1694, Newton paid his first visit to Flamsteed, sailing several miles to Greenwich in a small boat down the Thames. (This may have been the only time in his life that he journeyed by boat.) He wanted data about the motion of the moon, his current obsession. Newton needed Flamsteed's observations and basically took the astronomer's life's work and used it for his own benefit. Whatever data Flamsteed gave him, Newton wanted *more*, always accusing Flamsteed of holding back. During one screaming fight, Newton completely lost his cool and called the astronomer a "puppy."

Newton's next maneuver was to delay and sabotage the publication of Flamsteed's masterwork, a thorough cataloging of the stars. In 1712, as president of the Royal Society, Newton was able to force Flamsteed to surrender his charts and astronomical observations—thirty-five years of work—so that someone else could complete the book. Flamsteed was later able to acquire most of the printed copies (which had numerous errors), and he burned them.

After Flamsteed's death in 1719, loyal assistants completed his work in the form he had originally envisioned. When *British History of the Heavens* finally came out in 1725—more than twenty years after Flamsteed had hoped—it was recognized as a milestone of astronomy.

Newton was eighty-three by then, ailing, incontinent, still badmouthing the former Astronomer Royal to anyone who would listen.

CHAPTER EIGHT

The Greatest Science Book in the World

E WAS A MAN who was paranoid about divulging his own work and a man who begrudged and sabotaged the work of others. And yet in the final analysis, Newton redeemed himself because of a single work that he wrote and then published in 1687.

By the 1680s, it was generally agreed among the most up-to-date astronomers that the orbital paths of the planets were elliptical, as Kepler had described. But no one understood why.

One evening in January 1683, Newton's nemesis,

Robert Hooke, was in a coffeehouse in London, schmoozing with Edmond Halley and Christopher Wren on the subject of orbital paths. (Coffeehouses were all the rage, offering the stimulation of caffeine and talk—lots of talk.) Hooke, as was typical of him, acted as if he already had figured out why planets traveled in ellipses but didn't feel like sharing his answer. Halley became obsessed with solving it. Wren offered a large sum of money to whomever came up with the answer.

They decided that someone would have to make a pilgrimage to the only man in England who might know for sure—Isaac Newton. But who should go? Obviously not Hooke—Newton despised him. Neither Wren nor Halley had alienated Newton. Wren was still up to his ears in building projects after the London fire. So Halley was it. He cringed at the thought, but decided that flattery was the way to approach the hypersensitive professor.

The following August, Halley traveled to Cambridge to see Newton. Flattery worked. Newton understood exactly why orbits were elliptical, he told Halley. He had figured out the reason during his

"miracle year" at Woolsthorpe. He had even translated the orbital path into a mathematical formula.
He dug around his cluttered chambers, looking for
his calculations, promising to send them to Halley
later.

He did—and eventually sent Halley a nine-page
letter explaining elliptical orbits. The letter was the
basis of what eventually became three books that are
known by one title: *Philosophiae Naturalis Principia
Mathematica* (Mathematical Principles of Natural
Philosophy). The *Principia* is generally considered
one of the most important works *ever* in the history
of science.

Newton wrote all five hundred pages over a
period of eighteen months. He needed an assistant.
His longtime roommate and copyist, John Wickins,
was gone. The *Principia* was transcribed by a new
roommate and assistant, Humphrey Newton (no rela-
tion). A young student from his old grammar school
in Grantham, Humphrey served him for five years.
(These two did stay friendly; in later life, Humphrey
named his son Isaac in honor of his "dear deceased
friend.")

He is the only eyewitness to Newton's writing

of the *Principia*. He reported that Newton often forgot to eat during the project. He didn't even take time to sit down. He wrote standing up, taking a spoonful now and then of gruel or milk with eggs. When he did venture outside, he would pause, as if lost, and then disappear into his chambers again.

Ever-diplomatic Edmond Halley, in his capacity as Clerk of the Royal Society, deserves much credit for the publication of the *Principia*. Halley must have been quite the flatterer. He not only persuaded Newton to write it, holding his hand all through the process, but was able to keep Newton from stopping publication because of some advance criticism from Hooke.

Moreover, Halley paid for the cost of printing the *Principia* himself. The Royal Society was keenly interested in the book, but was nearly bankrupt and reluctant to finance it. They had been burned by poor sales of a two-volume *History of Fishes*. As for Halley, all he received for footing the bills on Newton's book was fifty leftover copies of *History of Fishes*.

So what makes the *Principia* such a landmark in scientific thinking? Three laws of motion form the basis of Newton's masterpiece. They describe how objects move, the way they bounce off each other, and what happens when they are pushed or pulled by outside forces.

The first is called the law of inertia. An object that isn't moving won't move unless an outside force puts it in motion. And once in motion, the object will keep on moving in a straight path unless another force changes it.

The second law states that the amount of force needed to move an object is determined by the mass of the object and also the amount that its speed changes while moving.

The third law, that every action has an equal and opposition reaction, is said to have occurred to Newton while observing billiard balls in play; when two balls collide, they bounce off in opposite direc- tions. Another way to visualize the third law is to picture a rocket—gases from burning fuel shooting out the back to push the rocket forward.

"From the same principles," he wrote grandly, "I now demonstrate the frame of the System of the World." His splendid unifying idea was his theory of gravitation: "All matter attracts all other matter with a force proportional to the product of their masses and inversely proportional to the square of the distance between them."

What does this mean? Every particle in the universe is attracted to, or exerts a tug on, every other particle. For example, you as an object are pulling all the objects around you into your own gravitational field. And at the same time, these objects are pulling on you. But the more massive that something is, the greater the force it will exert. An apple is much smaller than the earth, so the earth exerts a lot more force on the apple than vice versa. Still, when an apple falls, it actually pulls the earth toward it a little, just not enough to be noticed.

And the farther away two objects are, the weaker the force they exert on each other. The force gets weaker much faster than the change in distance. So if you double the distance between two objects, the attraction between them becomes four times weaker. If you triple the distance, the attraction becomes nine times weaker.

Other people had had vaguely similar ideas, but Newton was able to create an accurate mathematical equation that expressed the force. It is

$$F = \frac{G\, m_1\, m_2}{d^2}$$

In his equation, F=force, G=gravity, m_1=mass of the first object, m_2=mass of the second object, and d=distance.

Translated, this means that the pull of any two objects varies inversely as the square of the distance between them. So Newton called his equation "the inverse square law of attraction."

Endless applications can be derived from Newton's work. He could apply his laws to orbiting bodies, projectiles, pendulums, and free fall near the earth. This one principle explains why an apple falls to the ground and why the moon stays in its orbit around the earth—and why the tides ebb and flow, why the planets move as they do, and why humans don't fly into space as the earth rotates.

Much of this—like the inverse square law— Newton had worked out during his plague year at Woolsthorpe. Now he was going public in a big way.

It was all incredibly "elegant," a word scientists use to mean a truth stated as cleanly as possible. On top of everything else, he also laid out several rules for scientific reasoning. For example, we are to admit no more causes of natural things than are both true and sufficient to explain their appearances. In other words, keep it simple—don't grab at extra explana tions to say why something is so.

After outlining his rules for reasoning, he went on to describe in detail how they might be applied to solving any given problem: "The investigation of difficult things" ought to consist "of making experi ments and observations, and . . . drawing general con clusions from them by induction." A scientific law also had to be able to predict events. That was a sign of its validity. For instance, Newton's laws of motion predicted and accounted for strange observations in the sky (for example, why sometimes planets look from the earth as if they're moving backward).

Here was the summing up of something truly rev olutionary. We now call it the scientific method.

Newton, genius that he was, realized that even he would not find answers to all the questions he had. And he would make mistakes. So he reassured future scientists by admitting, "To explain all nature is too difficult a task for any one man, or even for any one age. 'Tis much better to do a little with certainty, and leave the rest for others that come after you, than to explain all things."

So his book was like a box of toys, with enough in it for all the thinkers who came after him to play with.

Does all this sound complicated? It was. Newton's laws are simple in the sense of being basic and universal. But "simple" doesn't mean easy. His book was very complicated. Newton had in fact *intentionally* made his book difficult to comprehend. He wanted "to avoid being baited by little smatterers in mathematics." ("Smatterers" was his insulting word for amateurish outsiders asking questions.) Plus, the *Principia* was written in Latin, the language of scholars. A popular joke around Cambridge was to point at Newton and say, "There goes a man that hath writ a book that neither he nor anyone else understands."

Five hundred copies of the *Principia* were printed. It finally appeared in the summer of 1687, when Newton was forty-five. He happily sent copies to everyone he knew. One copy went to King James II—a copy of every published book had to be sent to the king.

The *Principia* was hailed as a masterpiece, though hardly anyone actually read it. Noblemen offered large sums to anyone who could explain it to them. There were also seventeenth-century equivalents of "Newton for Dummies."

Others, like English philosopher John Locke, thought of him as a god. Newton insisted his results were not of divine revelation, but rather the culmination of years of solitary thinking—"due to nothing but industry and patient thought."

The *Principia* was not translated into English until 1729, two years after Newton died—due to lack of demand. Nevertheless, it was the first book on modern physics, the most fundamental of all natural sciences. Physics explains how the physical universe works—the basic laws of matter and energy and how they interact. Newton took known facts about the physical world and formed mathematical theories to explain them. He used his theories to predict the behavior of objects in all kinds of different circumstances, and then compared his predictions with what he observed in experiments. Finally, Newton used his results to check—and if need be, modify—his theories. His *Principia* was a broad statement that the world was ruled by mechanics. Yet this never made him question his underlying faith that the world was God's creation.

It took imagination of a rare order for someone to make these grand connections between things invisible to the naked eye. Newton's mind was open, creative, radiant, nearly impossible to explain.

As the famous eighteenth-century poet Alexander Pope phrased Newton's accomplishment,

Nature and Nature's laws lay hid in night;
God said, *Let Newton be!* and all was light.

CHAPTER NINE

Newton versus Newton

RILLIANT? ABSOLUTELY. BUT is Isaac
Newton an example of someone who was
both brilliant *and* several slices short of a loaf?

It may seem as though this fragile man was always
close to or in the midst of a breakdown. In the years
after the publication of the *Principia*, Newton
became—despite himself—a star, the first celebrity
scientist. It sounds as if, for a while, he was enjoying
himself. On occasion, he would even leave the sanctuary of Cambridge for London.

London was a smoky, unhealthy city of just under

a million, the majority living in dire poverty. But it was booming again after the Great Fire, with newspapers now speeding the flow of information. Newton became friendly with a whole host of young scientists and admirers, the people he formerly dismissed as "smatterers." With a brandnew confidence, he arranged to have the top artist in London paint his portrait—the first of *twenty* portraits.

In 1689 the university elected Newton one of their two members to Parliament. This had him journeying frequently to London. While he does not appear to have taken part in parliamentary debate— ever—he once asked the usher to close the window.

But then in the early 1690s, he finally had a fullblown collapse, a period of disabling depression. Opinions differ regarding the cause. Never given to selfanalysis, he left no clues.

It's possible there was a damaging fire. He went to chapel one winter morning, leaving a candle lit in his chambers. His dog may have knocked it over. The fire destroyed irreplaceable papers, years of work. A witness reported that when Newton came back from chapel, "everyone thought he would have run mad, he was so troubled thereat he was not himself for a month after." The fire is usually ascribed to 1693.

The taxing work of writing the *Principia* for pub-lication may have knocked him off balance. He had to know the book was going to permanently change his life—and perhaps he dreaded it. After so many years of seclusion in his dusty Cambridge quarters, he was exposed to the real world and to real people.

His life up until now hadn't exactly been bal-anced. Newton had no interest in music or art; he once dismissed poetry as "ingenious fiddle-faddle." He never exercised, had no hobbies or interest in games, and had no romantic attachment.

With one possible exception. In 1689 he met a twenty-five-year-old Swiss mathematician, Nicolas Fatio de Duillier. Their friendship became the closest personal relationship he ever experienced, with plen-ty of letters of genuine affection for Fatio, who in turn worshipped Newton. The intense friendship went on for four years. Newton invited Fatio to take rooms next to his in Cambridge. Then, like all his past associations, it was over—abruptly, mysteriously, and bitterly. Fatio was none too stable and later joined a sect of controversial mystics who were pilloried in London—literally pelted with eggs and rotten food.

Some scholars have speculated that their relationship was homosexual. There is no evidence one way or the other, just as there is no proof of the exact nature of his relationship with his roommate of twenty years, John Wickins. If Newton was homosexual, he most likely would have borne a heavy load of guilt. He would have had to keep any such relationship secret, since homosexual acts were against the law. Breaking off from Fatio in 1693 might have plunged him into a state of turmoil.

Whatever the cause, Newton's insomnia turned severe, and he began experiencing amnesia, loss of mental ability. How awful and frightening for a man whose main occupation was thinking. He began writing strange letters: "I must withdraw from your acquaintance and see neither you nor the rest of my friends anymore." This he wrote to the famous diarist and fellow Royal Society member Samuel Pepys.

He accused another friend, philosopher John Locke, of trying "to embroil me with women," adding that "when one told me you were sickly . . . I answered 'twere better if you were dead."

His friends realized he was ill—Pepys called it "a discomposure in the head"—and did not take Newton's harsh words to heart.

Later Newton apologized, trying to explain

himself: "When I wrote to you I had not slept an hour a night for a fortnight together and for five nights together not a wink." But he couldn't seem to dig deeper beyond blaming insomnia. Of vital concern to him was that he lacked "former consistency of mind." How was he going to keep working?

This was his longest period of what he called "dis-temper." Rumors spread of his ailment, and many assumed (or among enemies, hoped) he was perma-nently ill, his career over. Even on good days, Newton's life seemed outwardly joyless. Some wor-ried that he was literally killing himself with study.

Humphrey Newton, his assistant for five years, reported hearing him laugh only once (bitter mocking laughter after a "smatterer" asked him what use was Euclid's geometry book). As we've seen, criticism to Newton was like a match to a stick of dynamite. A colleague of Newton's, William Whiston, saw his rage up close: "Newton was of the most fearful, cau-tious and suspicious temper that I ever knew."

Even an admirer like Locke wrote diplomatically to a friend that Newton was "a little too apt to raise in himself suspicions where there is no ground." He suggested that if his friend had to ask Newton anything touchy, "pray do it with all the tenderness in the world."

Modern-day psychologists have tried to diagnose Newton from a distance of three centuries. Did his mother's abandonment, his lonely childhood warp him for life? Or did he battle chronic depression? Others believe he might have been bipolar, or a manic-depressive—a person who alternates between periods of extreme melancholy and overly "wired" activity.

Some recent researchers guess that Newton may have had Asperger syndrome, a form of autism that is associated with startling talents as well as crippling social "disabilities." We know he could focus for very long periods on his work and had a limited but intense range of interests. Yet socially he was like someone lost in a foreign land. He didn't seem to know how to make conversation, "read" people, or respond appropriately in situations.

It is impossible to know, after the fact, precisely what ailed him or what caused the crisis in 1693. But after some eighteen months, the black cloud lifted, and Newton regained his balance— such as it was.

CHAPTER TEN

And What about Alchemy?

*I*N RECENT YEARS, a few scholars have suggested yet another explanation for Newton's behavior. Newton may have suffered from toxic metal poisoning. In the 1970s, a lock of his hair was analyzed. His hair was found to contain mercury at forty times the expected normal level. Mercury poisoning can cause loss of appetite, insomnia, and mental instability.

Why would Newton's hair be full of mercury?

Because math and physics weren't the only subjects that occupied Newton's busy brain. He had another obsession that wasn't discovered until after he died. Alchemy.

Around 1669, Newton became obsessed with the processes by which one substance changes into another. The ultimate goal of this art—alchemy— was making the fabled Philosophers' Stone, which was believed to have the power to "purify" worth- less metals—in other words, turn them into gold. No wonder so many were intrigued—the stone, it was whispered, did everything from making gold to extending life and curing disease. Readers of *Harry Potter and the Sorcerer's Stone* will recognize this as the much-coveted "Stone" of the title. (The British edition is actually called *Harry Potter and the Philosopher's Stone*.)

By Newton's time, alchemy was discredited, illegal. At least one member of the Royal Society was imprisoned for it.

Chemistry—the science that deals with the prop- erties, composition, and structure of substances—was in its infancy. In 1661, Robert Boyle published *The Sceptical Chymist*, a landmark work on the new rational and testable chemistry. He gave the first pre- cise definitions of a chemical element (a substance that cannot be broken down further), a chemical reaction, and chemical analysis, and made studies of acids and bases.

As a student at Cambridge, Newton studied Boyle. Much later he went on to publish a two-page chemistry paper, *On the Nature of Acids*. But there is little question that his passion was alchemy. He carried out hundreds of experiments and left over a million words on how to turn base metals into precious ones. He spent far more time on these pursuits than on physics or math or light.

Newton's was the first laboratory at Cambridge University. He installed elaborate experimental apparatus in a shed in the garden outside his and Wickins's rooms—two furnaces that burned at all times, a chimney he built to carry away smoke and noxious fumes, glass equipment, and metal cauldrons. And chemicals—mercury, sulfur, aqua fortis (nitric acid), arsenic, lead, and many others, some smelly, some poisonous.

He started with a copy of the standard book on alchemy, the *Theatrum Chemicum*—all six heavy volumes. He made special trips to London, taking the coach to the Swan Tavern on Grays Inn Lane,

then walking to booksellers who carried titles he was looking for. He would meet secretly with fellow alchemists. He ended up with 138 books on alchemy, the most comprehensive collection of his day. He read every book in print as well as unpublished manu-scripts, some written in riddles and codes, which he or an assistant would put in long hours deciphering and copying.

Ironically, at the same time he balked at writing letters to math "smatterers," he was eager to corre-spond with alchemists. Even with them, he used a secret name—*Jeova sanctus unus*, an anagram for *Isaacus Neutonus*. It meant "God's holy one." To those outside the field, he was always circumspect about this other interest, making vague excuses— "Being desirous to prosecute some other subjects . . ." "business of my own . . ." "having other things in my head."

Always reckless in experimenting on himself, he used to "taste test" his own mixtures. He was breathing in fumes of melting metals at times, and some type of poisoning could have occurred. Newton's ailments do fit in with self-induced mer-cury poisoning. On the other hand, there is not

much evidence that he had a tremor, the most common and telltale sign. Loose teeth are another
symptom, but he kept all of his teeth except one.
And he lived to a ripe old age, in relative good
health. Mercury poisoning can't be proved;
nonetheless, it is interesting as a possible explanation for Newton's depression and emotional crisis.
Whatever its effects, for thirty years Newton
experimented with alchemy. After his death, scholars who found the material were shocked. "Not fit
to be printed," they wrote.

What prompted the obsession? We still don't
know. Was it the lure of creating gold, a hunger for
wealth left from his days as a subsizar? Was his interest first stimulated by concocting potions in the
apothecary's shop in Grantham? Or the appeal of
secret knowledge available to a select few? Or the
lure of a puzzle that hadn't been solved? Surely he
would be the one to crack the code? Was he approach-
ing science from every possible angle—no matter how
strange—in his zeal to understand the nature and
structure of all matter?

Or was his purpose in studying alchemy a religious one? An alchemist was called an "adept," a

gifted person touched by God. Alchemists liked to think of themselves as "priests of nature," distinguished by their wisdom and purity. Some believed that the precious Philosophers' Stone had spiritual powers, that it made communication with angels possible, that it could be used as a weapon against atheists, or unbelievers.

We know God was never out of Newton's mind. Nothing he discovered ever shook his faith. "In the absence of any other proof, the thumb alone would convince me of God's existence," he once wrote. The whole purpose of science was to exalt God. A witness reported that Newton's usually "melancholy and thoughtful" face would turn "lightsome and cheerful" during talk of religion, as if he was "transported."

Interpreting the Bible was yet another one of his obsessions discovered only after his death. As with alchemy, this too was top-secret work, because his readings weren't traditional. One particular concern was to work out an elaborate timeline of Earth's history from clues in the Bible, Greek mythology, and various ancient arcane texts. But his fixation was prophecy—the determination of future events from correct interpretation of biblical passages.

He was obsessed to the point of mania with the idea of the end of the world. He finally decided upon a date—the year 2060—which he jotted down on scrap paper found long after his death.

In 2003, his choice of 2060 as the end of the world became news. It was the sort of story one would expect to see on the covers of supermarket tabloids.

Newton's religious beliefs almost cost him his university career. In 1675, to retain his pleasant professorship in mathematics, he was required to become ordained in the Church of England. Once again, he would have to swear under oath that he believed in the Holy Trinity. But he wasn't going to do it. Not this time. Even though he had planted deep roots at Cambridge, he was prepared to resign.

At the last moment, Newton was exempted from taking holy orders. We don't know exactly why. Such a dispensation had to come from very high up—the king or someone closely connected to him. It was probably Newton's old math professor Isaac Barrow who came to his aid. Barrow may have argued that Newton did not exactly have the social skills to be a clergyman.

So Newton held on to his professorship, and when he finally left Cambridge, it was his own decision to move on.

CHAPTER ELEVEN
The Crimson Years

RINITY COLLEGE BEGAN having financial problems, and Newton was not being paid regularly. He'd been connected with Cambridge for thirty-five years, yet now he decided to pull up his deep roots and move to London, a more intellectually inviting place.

He took a job in London, a job that dealt with money. In 1696, through a friend in a high place, Newton was appointed Warden of the Mint. At first he shrank from such "vexatious" work, but then he threw himself into it. He was so driven to do well that he was promoted to Master of the Mint, a post that he held for twenty-seven years—the rest of his life.

Parliament had set up the first central bank, the Bank of England, in 1694. Paper money was not in everyday use. To the average person, money meant coins. Every day Newton went off to work in the Tower of London. He was in charge of the complete reform of England's coinage. A common practice was to clip the edges off silver and gold coins, making them weigh less so they were worth less than their marked value. Coins were reminted with ribbed edges so that any clipping would be instantly apparent.

Not only was Newton's post well paid, but he even got a commission on the amount of money minted. All the gold and silver of the realm were his to control. It was also part of his job to prosecute counterfeiters, which he did with cruel diligence. He sent twenty-seven forgers to the hangman in just one year—and he was always there at the gallows attending the executions, though it wasn't required of him.

As a highly paid government official, Newton

lived with his niece in a house on Jermyn Street, in London's West End. It was a life of comfort and dignity. He had a coach and six servants, and not one but two chamber pots made of solid silver. His library contained over two thousand books. His menus included geese, turkeys, rabbit, barrels of beer, and bottles of wine. His favorite pleasure was eating apples, boiled orange peels, and roasted quince.

One visitor to Newton's house noted the luxurious furniture and the "atmosphere of crimson"— the draperies, the mohair bed with curtains, the couches were all in crimson. Newton himself wore velvety red robes.

He actually became . . . plump. People said they saw him smile and even laugh, though he was still known as a man of exceptionally few words, still studious and serious. He hadn't undergone a complete personality transplant.

As soon as his least favorite person (Robert Hooke) died, Newton became active in the Royal Society again. In 1703 he was elected president—a formidable one, something of a tyrant. It is said that one of his first actions was to have Hooke's portrait removed from the building and Hooke's papers destroyed. Newton's paramount concern was always protecting and polishing his own reputation, often in petty ways.

Of late, the Society's focus had drifted, and it was becoming more and more an object of ridicule. Members debated which time of day was best to smell flowers, what happened if you drank a pint of cow urine, and what poisons were being used in murder cases. Newton brought the focus back to serious science. "I do not deal in conjectures," he once declared. He missed only three meetings during the next twenty years. Anyone who crossed him was out. During his reign, the Society worked on practical problems like the building of a water pump, improving farming practices, and even the invention of a "sailing chariot"—a horseless carriage that would move by wind.

With Hooke safely dead, Newton brought out his second great book, *Opticks*, in 1704. It included his theories of light and color discovered so long ago. It was more accessible and had a wider audience than the *Principia*.

In 1705, Queen Anne knighted Newton—a political maneuver, but unheard-of attention for a figure in science. The impressive ceremony took place in the great dining hall at Cambridge, where Sir Isaac had once waited tables.

He ended his days hanging out with King George II and Queen Caroline, giving stately dinner parties, telling distinguished visitors the story of the apple. These years were gossip-free except for the affair his niece had with the man who had got Newton his cushy job at the mint. Newton reportedly spent hours every sunny morning blowing soap bubbles through a clay pipe, not playing, but examining.

At the time of his death, he was hard at work on *The Chronology of Ancient Kingdoms Amended*, his biblical chronology. Cleansed of any heresy, it came out a year after his death but is definitely not what Newton is remembered for.

He died at age eighty-five in 1727. It was a painful death from gout, lung inflammation, and kidney stones. He apparently turned down painkillers, though opium would have been legally available to him back then.

In his final moments, he made one last character-istic gesture of rebellion. Knowing he was dying, he

refused to receive the Last Sacrament. At the time no one understood why. But it must have been on the grounds that it would violate his personal and unorthodox beliefs. Eccentric, stubborn, against the mainstream to the end.

He was buried in Westminster Abbey, the first scientist to be so honored. At his huge funeral, so full of pomp it was worthy of a king, speakers hailed him as "the glory of the British nation." His monument reads, "Let mortals rejoice that there has existed such and so great an ornament of the human race."

CHAPTER TWELVE

Impact

*A*FTER HIS DEATH, Newton's fame continued to soar. He went from superstar to
megastar, his name a synonym for smartness. Busts of
Newton became de rigueur in the parlors of middle-
class homes; important men like Benjamin Franklin,
when having their portraits painted, made sure a bust
of Newton was in the background.

The well-known French philosopher Voltaire was
responsible, in large part, for publicizing Newton's
work and burnishing his reputation. Scientifically,
Voltaire was not an expert, but his partner, a woman

named Gabrielle-Émilie du Châtelet, was an accomplished mathematician and physicist. She translated
the *Principia* into French and brought a brand-new
audience to Newton's masterpiece. That book, all
by itself, is seen as a cornerstone of the Scientific
Revolution, the term for the period that saw an
explosion in scientific discovery. It began with
Copernicus, gathered steam with Galileo, and burst
with full force by the early 1700s. From Newton's
time on, science was the engine driving the modern
world.

Newton is important not only for what he
discovered but also for the way in which he
worked. He is often credited with introducing the
scientific method, or at least for stating its principles
explicitly. "I do not feign (make up) hypotheses,"
he stated. By this he meant that a hypothesis, an
explanation that accounts for why an event occurs,
must rely on evidence. The evidence must be tested
and tested again. If the hypothesis holds, then it
progresses to a "theory" and finally may be pro-
nounced a scientific "law."

Here is another way to understand the scientific
method.

One apple falls to the ground—that's a factual event. But it says only that something happened, not why or how. After more observations and experiments and a lot of thinking, Newton came up with the theory of gravity. That theory says all apples will always fall to the ground, and it explains why. The more a theory explains, the better it is. Newton's gravity theory explains not only the motion of apples but also those of planets, stars, moons, rocketships, skydivers. It's a terrific theory because it explains not only how things act, but how they will *always* act. All motion in the universe obeys the same law of gravitation—from the simple cycle of a washing machine to the flying of a spaceship to Mars.

Newton's procedures went on to be incorporated into chemistry, biology, every branch of science.

And after Newton, science became cool—actually fashionable. The average person was *supposed* to be interested in it now. People flocked to coffeehouses to hear lectures on different areas of science. A book called *Sir Isaac Newton's Philosophy Explain'd for the Use of the Ladies* encouraged women not to be afraid of science. There was even a children's book about

Newton, "adapted to the capacities of young gentle-men and ladies."

No longer was the Royal Society the *only* place in England dedicated to discussing science. Many other societies sprang up—the Medical, Zoological, Geological, and Meteorological Societies. Charles Babbage helped establish the Astronomical Society in 1820, going on to create the "Difference Engine"—the world's first computer. Thirteen years later, the British Association for the Advancement of Science finally coined the word "scientist" to replace the term "natural philosopher."

By 1826, the first university in London was estab-lished—training doctors and engineers, with science as a separate discipline. Women were allowed limited entry in 1869. It was generally understood that sci-ence could improve the quality of life—in medicine and technology in all sorts of unforeseen ways.

In England, this was the beginning of a steady, desperately needed rise in people's standard of living. Now England, speeding ahead in science, was poised to become the mighty British Empire, taking over and dominating one-fourth of the globe.

So who stands on Newton's shoulders? Everyone.

It cannot be said more plainly than that. Newton's work influenced everyone who came after him. Scientists did not see a need to tinker with Newtonian physics until the early twentieth century when the German physicist Albert Einstein came up with his masterwork, the theory of relativity. Newton's laws worked very well for most day-to-day situations. However, when Einstein started to wonder about extreme situations—for instance, what happened when something was traveling at the speed of light— he found that Newton's equations gave him answers that didn't make sense. To answer the questions he was asking, Einstein had to come up with a new way of thinking—his theory of relativity—that moved beyond Newtonian physics.

Yes, Newtonian physics has its limits, but there would be no Einstein without Newton. Indeed, Einstein called Newton the greatest genius of all time. Einstein wrote, "Nature to him was an open book, whose letters he could read without effort. . . . He stands before us strong, certain and alone."

Whatever his weird habits, Isaac Newton is generally credited with contributing more to the development of science than any other individual in

history. Newton himself summed up his accomplishments with uncharacteristic sweetness and light: "I
do not know what I may appear to the world; but to
myself I seem to have been only like a boy playing on
the seashore, and diverting myself in now and then
finding a smoother pebble or a prettier shell than ordi-
nary, whilst the great ocean of truth lay all undiscov-
ered before me."

For a man who never actually saw the seashore,
someone who traveled endlessly in his imagination but
only 150 miles in real life, Isaac Newton expanded
everyone's horizons.

BIBLIOGRAPHY

(* books or magazine articles especially for young readers)

Ackroyd, Peter. *London: The Biography.* New York: Doubleday, 2000.

* Anderson, Margaret J. *Isaac Newton: The Greatest Scientist of All Time.* Berkeley Heights, New Jersey: Enslow, 1996.

Aughton, Peter. *Newton's Apple: Isaac Newton and the English Scientific Renaissance.* London: Weidenfeld & Nicholson, 2003.

Berlinski, David. *Newton's Gift: How Sir Isaac Newton Unlocked the System of the World.* New York: The Free Press, 2000.

* Christianson, Gale E. *Isaac Newton and the Scientific Revolution.* New York: Oxford University Press, 1996.

Fara, Patricia. *Newton: The Making of Genius.* New York: Columbia University Press, 2002.

Gleick, James. *Isaac Newton.* New York: Pantheon Books, 2003.

Hellman, Hal. *Great Feuds in Science.* New York: John Wiley & Sons, Inc., 1998.

Jardine, Lisa. *The Curious Life of Robert Hooke: The Man Who Measured London.* New York: HarperCollins, 2004.

Merton, Robert K. *Science, Technology & Society in Seventeenth-Century England.* New York: Howard Fertig, Inc., 2001.

* **Principe, Lawrence.** "The Philosophers' Stone," *Muse* magazine, February 2004.

Westfall, Richard S. *The Life of Isaac Newton.* Cambridge, United Kingdom: Cambridge University Press, 1993.

White, Michael. *Isaac Newton: The Last Sorcerer.* Reading, Massachusetts: Addison-Wesley, 1997.

WEB SITES
(Verified July 2005)

"Footprints of the Lion: Isaac Newton at Work," Cambridge University:
http://www.lib.cam.ac.uk/Exhibitions/Footprints_of_the_Lion/

"Isaac Newton: Theology, Prophecy, Science and Religion," the Newton
Project Canada: http://www.isaac-newton.org/

The Isaac Newton Resources Page of the Isaac Newton Institute
for Mathematical Sciences: http://www.newton.cam.ac.uk/newton.html.
(Links to online resources concerning Newton's life, work, and
manuscripts)

"The Newtonian Moment: Science and the Making of Modern
Culture," New York Public Library exhibit:
http://www.nypl.org/research/newton/

"The Newton Project," Imperial College, London:
http://www.newtonproject.ic.ac.uk/index.html (Newton's manuscripts,
including his three college notebooks)

"The Royal Society": http://www.royalsoc.ac.uk

"Trinity College, Cambridge": http://www.trin.cam.ac.uk/

INDEX

academic careers, 44; *see also* fellowships, university
alchemy, 38, 95–96, 100
  books on, 96
  defined, 95
  illegality of, 95
  Newton's reasons for studying, 99
algebra, 50
almanac, 26
American colonies, 40, 74
amnesia, 91
analytical geometry, 38
Anglican Church, *see* Church of England
Anne, Queen, 106
annus mirabilis, 53, 69, 79, 83
apothecary, 21, 99
apple, story of Newton and, 13, 16, 18, 107
apples, falling, 11, 48, 82, 83, 112
applications of Newton's work, 83, 84, 112
Aristotle, 35–36, 37, 41, 51, 52
arithmetic, 23; *see also* mathematics
Asperger syndrome, 93
astrology, 40
Astronomer Royal, England's first, 74
astronomical observations, 40, 44, 75
Astronomical Society, 113
astronomy, 35, 36–37, 40, 57, 74–76
autism, 93

Babbage, Charles, 113
bachelor's degree, 44
Bacon, Francis, 38–39, 41
Bank of England, 104
Barrow, Isaac, 40, 69, 101–2
  as mentor, 39, 57
Bate, John, 26
"Bedlam" (Bethlehem Hospital), 61
Bible, 16
  interpretation of, 100, 107
  study of, 23, 35
Black Death, *see* bubonic plague
boats, 75

books, 17, 18, 22, 26, 32, 56, 105
  on alchemy, 98
Boyle, Robert, 95, 96
British Association for the Advancement of Science, 113
British Empire, 113
British History of the Heavens, 75
British Navy, 74
bubonic plague, 22, 44, 46, 53
  Newton's medicine for, 47
  no cure for, 46
  outbreak of 1348, 45
  symptoms, 45
busts of Newton, 110

calculus, 67, 70
  defined, 50–51, 68
  different systems of symbols, 50, 69, 70
  invention of, 11, 50, 69, 70–71
Calculus Priority Dispute, 69, 70–71
  Royal Society committee rules on, 71–73
calendar reform, 26
Cambridge University, 16, 22, 30, 54, 55, 90, 101, 102, 107
  closed by plague, 46
  curriculum, 34–35, 36, 39
  Newton as fellow at, 12, 54–55, 58–59
  Newton leaves, 103
  Newton as student at, 36, 39, 43
card-playing, 34, 56
Caroline, Queen, 107
cat, Newton's, 43
Catholic Church, 37
cattle, 16
cause and effect, 41
celebrity, 88, 110, 112
celibacy, 55
chapel, 58, 89
Charles I beheaded, 12, 17
Charles II, 17, 57
chemical element, definition of, 95–96
chemistry, 39, 95–96, 112